BMX &
MOUNTAIN BIKING

Frances Ridley

Editorial Consultant – Cliff Moon

RISING★STARS

nasen
NASEN House, 4/5 Amber Business Village, Amber Close,
Amington, Tamworth, Staffordshire B77 4RP

Rising Stars UK Ltd.
22 Grafton Street, London W1S 4EX
www.risingstars-uk.com

Every effort has been made to trace copyright holders and obtain their permission for use of copyright material. The publisher will gladly receive information enabling them to rectify any error or omission in subsequent editions.

All facts are correct at time of going to press.

Published 2006

Cover design: Button plc
Cover image: Ron Chapple/Alamy
Illustrator: Bill Greenhead
Text design and typesetting: Nicholas Garner, Codesign
Technical advisers: Phil Braybrooke, Jill and Steve Behr
Educational consultants: Cliff Moon and Lorraine Petersen
Pictures: Stockfile: pages 5, 6, 7, 16, 20, 21, 24, 25, 26, 27, 28, 29, 32, 33. Alamy: 4, 10, 38. Buzz Pictures: pages 11, 12, 16. Corbis: pages 13, 15. Getty Images: pages 14, 17. FreezeFrame: page 22. Justin Kosman: page 9. Free Agent BMX: page 8

British Library Cataloguing in Publication Data.
A CIP record for this book is available from the British Library.

ISBN: 1-905056-90-7

Printed by Craft Print International Ltd, Singapore

This book should not be used as a guide to the sports shown in it. The publishers accept no responsibility for any harm which might result from taking part in these sports. ALWAYS wear a helmet and do not attempt any of the stunts shown without supervision.

Contents

BMX and mountain bikes

BMX and mountain biking started in **California** in the 1960s and 1970s.

Bike riders began racing on off-road tracks.

They called the new sport 'bicycle motocross' – or BMX.

The first BMX riders **customised** their bikes.

Soon, companies started to make BMX bikes.

Bike riders began racing down steep hills.
They used one-gear bikes called 'clunkers'.

An early Breezer mountain bike

Champ Facts!

Gary Fisher was one of the first mountain bikers.

In 1979, he started a company called MountainBikes which sold bikes for downhill racing.

Now, many companies make mountain bikes.

BMX racing

The races

A BMX race is called a moto.

The riders race around a short track.
Up to eight riders race in each moto.

BMX races are short.
It's important to get a good start.

The riders line up behind a start gate.

The race starts when the gate drops.

The riders race downhill and into the first turn.

BMX tracks have corners, **berms** and jumps.

BMX berm

Riders race down the final straight as fast as they can.

The bikes

BMX racing bikes are strong, fast and light.

This bike is a Free Agent Team Limo.

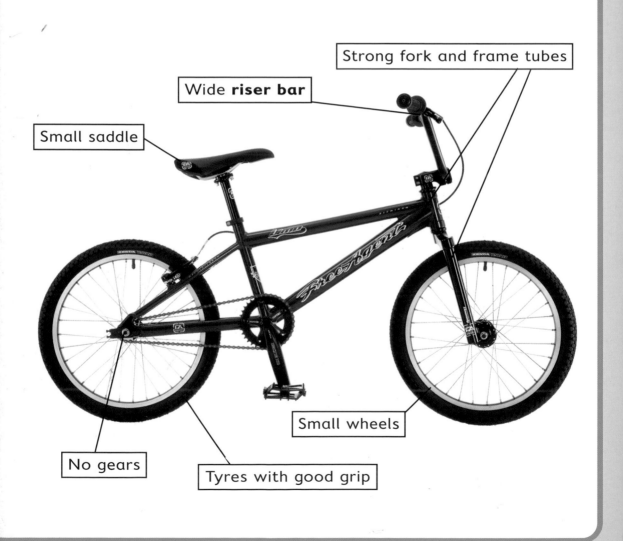

Strong fork and frame tubes

Wide **riser bar**

Small saddle

Small wheels

No gears

Tyres with good grip

The teams and riders

BMX teams are run by companies that make BMX bikes.

The teams **sponsor** the riders in BMX events.

Free Agent

Top rider Kyle Bennett rides for Free Agent.
He has won races on the Team Limo bike.

Fact!
Kyle Bennet's nickname is 'Butter'.

Kyle Bennet was **UCI** World Champion in 2002 and 2003.

BMX stunt riding

BMX riders used to do stunts between motos.

Some riders liked the stunts better than the racing.

Now, there are lots of different kinds of stunt riding.

Flatlanders balance on their bikes.

Vert riders use ramps to jump with their bikes.

Dirt jumpers go round a run with lots of jumps.

Street riders do stunts on things they find in the street.

Park riders do stunts in stunt parks.

Flatland

Flatland riders balance on one part of the bike.

They move the bike around by twisting it or **scuffing** it.

Flatland riders link moves together.

They lose points if their feet touch the ground.

Endo

Tailwhip

Flatland bikes are easy to move around. They are small, light and strong.

Flatland bikes have front and rear brakes.

The handlebars turn all the way round.

Short frame

Lots of spokes

Stunt pegs

Smooth tyres

Champ Fact!

Terry Adams was the Flatland Champion of the 2005 **X Games.**

This stunt is a double-seat grab.

Vert and dirt

Vert riders and dirt jumpers do tricks in the air.

Vert riders ride up and down a wooden ramp.

They turn all the way round when they jump.

Fact!

Vert is short for 'vertical'.

Champ Fact!

Jamie Bestwick was the **X Games** 'Vert' and 'Vert Best Trick' Champion for 2005.

Strong, long frame

High seat

Big handlebars

Lots of spokes

Four pegs

Smooth tyres

Vert bikes are fast and strong. They have front and rear brakes. The handlebars turn all the way round.

Dirt jumpers ride around a dirt track.

They go from jump to jump.

Champ Fact!

Corey Bohan was the 2005 X Games Dirt Champion.

Dirt bikes are like vert bikes but they don't have front brakes or smooth tyres

Street and park

Street riders do tricks on things they find in the street.

- They bunnyhop stairs.

- They grind rails.

- They ride up walls and fences.

Park riders go to stunt parks to do tricks.

Park and street bikes are fast and easy to move.

Dave Mirra was the **X Games** 2005 Street/Stunt Park Champion.

It was his 13th gold medal at the X Games!

Dave Mirra is one of the best BMX riders.

Champ Fact!

Mirra's nickname is 'Miracle Boy'

Two pegs

Swept-back handlebars

Bike Wars – Cal

I hate mountain bikes – and anyone that rides them!

Take Ryan. We were mates years ago.

Then he went to some posh school.

That was thc last I saw of him – until Saturday.

I was in town doing tricks on my bike. Then I saw Ryan on his mountain bike. He rode over.

"Hi, Cal! Great to see you again."

Oh yeah? I didn't say anything.

"I like your bike," he said. "You're doing some great tricks."

"Yeah? Well, I don't like your bike," I said.

Cal looked hurt. I grinned – but then I saw Faye's face.

"Cal!" she said. "Hi, Ryan. It's good to see you!"

I went to the top of the steps and did a grind down the rail.

"Bet you can't do that!" I yelled.

Continued on page 30

19

Downhill racing

Downhill racers start at the top of a steep course.

They race down one at a time.

The rider with the fastest time is the winner.

Bikes can go faster than 50 mph.

Racers have to control their bikes at these speeds.

They have to think and act fast.

Downhill mountain bikes

Downhill bikes are fast and strong.

They need good suspension and strong brakes.

Downhill bikes are better at going down hills than up them! This is because they are very heavy.

Giant Glory downhill full suspension

Strong frame

Wide, high **riser bar**

Long travel rear suspension

Long travel front fork

Platform pedals

Big tyres with lots of grip

Strong **disc brakes**

Interview with Sam Dale

Sam Dale is a downhill racer.
He was the National Downhill Champion
for his age group in 2004/2005.

NAME: Sam Dale

DATE OF BIRTH: February 1990

BEST RESULT: Winning the National Points Series
and the Midlands Series

MAIN SPONSOR: Goldtec

1 How did you get into downhill racing?

I got into downhill racing when I was racing cross country. I saw downhill racing and I wanted to do it.

2 How do you get ready for a race?

I get to the track early. I walk the track first and then I ride it on my bike. I do fitness work before a race — weights and cross country rides.

3 What do you like about downhill?

Winning is great but I just love riding. My favourite tracks are Rheola in South Wales, Molefre Hall in North Wales and Fort William in Scotland.

4 What is your ambition in downhill racing?

To have fun and become professional.

Freeriding

Freeriders go anywhere and do anything!

Freeriders go downhill and uphill.

They ride off very high drops.

Riding off drops is called 'hucking'.

Josh Bender

Josh Bender has made his name in freeride videos.

He hucks off some very big drops!

He uses a bike with 30cm of **travel**.

Most freeride bikes don't have this much travel.

Freeriders also ride along very narrow posts.

Norco VPS A-line

Strong but **light-weight** frame

Long travel suspension fork

Light-weight saddle

Rear suspension

Gears

Strong **disc brake** with large rotor

Cross country racing

Mountain bike cross country racing is called XC.

XC is the only mountain bike sport in the Olympics.

Julien Absalon won the Olympic gold medal in 2004.

He won the MTB World Championship title in the same year.

Champ Fact!

Absalon wore a gold helmet and gold shoes for the World Championship. He even rode a gold bike!

A cross-country course has hills, trees, rocks and water.

The riders do about six laps of the course.

A race is about 40 km long and takes about two hours to complete.

Cross country mountain bikes

There are two kinds of XC mountain bikes.

XC full suspension bikes

These bikes have front and rear suspension but are still much lighter than a downhill bike.

They are heavier than hardtails but they are easier to ride.

Scott Genius 30

High saddle

Short travel rear suspension

Flat, narrow handlebars

XC hardtails

These bikes don't have rear suspension.

They are **light-weight** but harder to ride.

Many pro riders ride hardtails because they are faster.

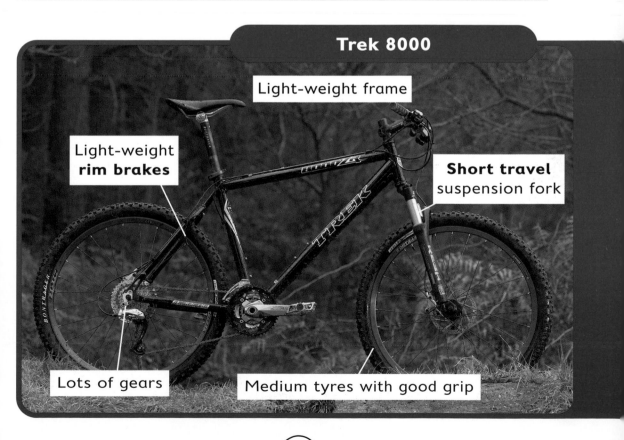

Trek 8000

Light-weight frame

Light-weight **rim brakes**

Short travel suspension fork

Lots of gears

Medium tyres with good grip

Bike Wars – Faye

Cal and Ryan used to be good mates.

Not any more.

Cal has dared Ryan to a contest next Saturday.

I've given Ryan my bike for the week.

Cal has been out on the bike every day.

He's doing some great tricks. But I wish he was doing them for fun.

It's more like a war or something.

Bike Wars – Ryan

I don't get Cal anymore.

We used to be mates.

We used to have fun.

I said yes to the contest so maybe we can be mates again.

I've learned some cool tricks on Faye's bike.

Street isn't my thing – XC is what I am good at.

But street is fun. Cal can do some great stuff.

Maybe he'll give me some tips when the contest is over.

Continued on page 34

Enduro events

Enduro events are long distance XC races.

Some enduros are on long courses.

Other enduros are on short courses.

The riders do as many laps as they can in a set time.
Many riders work in teams and take turns to ride.

Enduro Fact!

Some enduro events don't have a set course.

Riders use maps to find checkpoints.

Champ Fact!

John Stamstad was the first person to ride the '24 Hours of Canaan' solo.

The race was a relay – so he entered it four times under different names!

Bike Wars – The Contest

Ryan and I met outside the library. It's a great place for bikes.

Lots of kids turned up. I love crowds and I love doing tricks. I started the contest.

I bunnyhopped down the steps. Then I did some wheelies and endos.

I rode up the wall and did a grind down the rail. I ended with the best tailwhip ever.

The kids clapped and cheered.

They shouted my name.

"Cal! Cal! Cal!"

It felt great.

"Beat that, Ryan!" I said.

It felt like he was my mate again – I was in such a good mood!

He grinned. "I'll try!" he said, "But that was cool!"

He got on his bike.

The crowd didn't cheer. The kids were from *my* school. They wanted me to win.

Continued on the next page

Then Faye shouted out.

"Go for it, Ryan!"

It's funny – I wasn't mad at her.

I wasn't even mad at Ryan.

Ryan started with some wheelies. Then he did a big drop off the wall.

He rode along the bench and he did a track-stand – but he didn't hold it for long.

It was good – the kids cheered.

"That was great!" I said. "How long have you been doing tricks?"

"A week!" he said. "I need some tips, Cal!"

Faye came up.

"I won!" I told her. "I did the best tricks."

"Hang on!" said Ryan. "My tricks were cool."

"Maybe you need another contest," said Faye.

"OK," said Ryan. "But only if it's XC!"

"You're on!" said Cal.

Mountain bikes meet BMX!

Mountain bikes and BMX bikes have grown up together.

BMX bikes have borrowed things from mountain bikes and mountain bikes have borrowed things from BMX bikes.

Four mountain bike sports have strong links with BMX.

These are duel slalom, BSX, dirt jumping and trials.

Duel slalom

A duel slalom race starts with two lanes. You can move out of your lane near the finish!

There is only one fast line to the finish.

Both riders want to race that line — so there are lots of crashes!

BSX

BSX is short for Bicycle Super Cross.

It's like BMX racing – but downhill!

BSX courses are man-made.

They have corners, berms and huge jumps!

Dirt jumping

Mountain bike dirt jumping is like BMX dirt jumping.

Dirt jumpers link lots of jumps into a trail.

Sometimes they do tricks when they jump.

Sometimes they go round the course as smoothly as they can.

Super-strong bikes!

The bikes used for these sports are very, very strong!

Saracen Xess

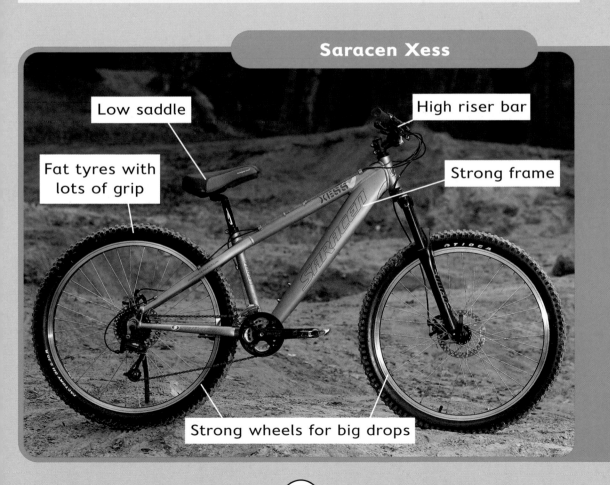

Low saddle

High riser bar

Fat tyres with lots of grip

Strong frame

Strong wheels for big drops

Trials

Trial riders have to get round a course without putting their feet down.

They jump along on their back wheels.
This is called 'hip hopping'.

Most **formal** competitions are held in the countryside.

The riders use logs, stumps, rocks and boulders.

Champ Fact!

Danni Comas was the 2005 World Bike Trial Champion.

Trials bikes are **light-weight** and strong.
Some trials bikes don't even have a saddle!

Koxx

Strong, light-weight frame

Big tyres with lots of grip

No front suspension

Large **platform pedals** with lots of grip

Quiz

1   Where did BMX and mountain biking start?

2   What were the first mountain bikes called?

3   What is another name for a BMX race?

4   What is Kyle Bennet's nickname?

5   What does 'scuffing' mean?

6   What is Sam Dale's ambition?

7   What is the only mountain bike sport in the Olympic Games?

8   What are the two kinds of XC mountain bike?

9   What type of event is a long distance XC race?

10 Name the 2005 World BikeTrial Champion.

Glossary of terms

berm	A banked corner.
California	State in the US.
customised	Changed to do its job better.
disc brake	Brake on the hub of the wheel.
formal	Follows set-down rules.
light-weight	Not heavy.
obstacles	Things that are in the way.
platform pedals	A flat surface for the foot. There are different kinds of platform pedals.
rim brake	Brake on the rim of the wheel.
riser bar	Handlebars with grips that are higher above the ground than the middle.
scuffing	Using your feet on the tyres of a bike to move or stop it.
sponsor	Company or person that gives riders money. In return, the rider has to wear or ride his sponsor's products.
travel	Distance that the wheel can move up and down from the frame.
UCI	Holds MTB and BMX competitions.
X Games	Competition for extreme sports.

More resources

Books

BMX Biking, Uncle Buck, Radical Sports Series, Heinemann Library
(0-43103-695-0)

Mountain Biking, Kirk Bizley, Radical Sports Series, Heinemann
Library (0-43103-676-4)

These two books are good for beginners. They tell you how to get
started, how to do tricks and how to keep safe.

Magazines

Mountain Biking UK, Future Publishing
This is the UK's biggest-selling mountain bike magazine. It has lots
of news, tips and great pictures.

Ride BMX, Transworld Publishing
A best-selling magazine that will keep you up-to-date with the world
of BMX.

Websites

http://www.bmxonline.com/bmx/
Ride BMX online

http://www.mbuk.com/text.asp?id=7
Mountain Biking UK online

These are the online versions of Ride BMX and Mountain Biking UK
magazines.

DVDs

Counterparts (2005) Duke Marketing Ltd (Cat. No. VHOT6740)
Lots of urban riding and dirt jumping – with a bit of downhill too!

Fundamentals (2004) Duke Marketing Ltd (Cat. No. VHOT6728)
All the advice you need to get you started in mountain biking.

Answers

1 California

2 Clunkers

3 Moto

4 'Butter'

5 Using your feet on the tyres of a bike to move or stop it

6 To have fun and become professional

7 Cross country

8 Hardtail and full suspension

9 An enduro

10 Danni Comas

Index